Trade

Steck Vaughn™

HOUGHTON MIFFLIN HARCOURT
Supplemental Publishers

www.SteckVaughn.com
800-531-5015

Trade

Trade
Fact Matters

ISBN-13: 978-1-4190-5480-8
ISBN-10: 1-4190-5480-5

First published by Blake Education Pty Ltd as *Go Facts*
Copyright © 2006 Blake Publishing
This edition copyright under license from Blake Education Pty Ltd
© 2010 Steck-Vaughn, an imprint of HMH Supplemental Publishers Inc.

Printed in China

2 3 4 5 6 7 8 0940 15 14 13 12 11 10

What Is Trade?

*Trade is the exchange of **goods** or **services**. Trade can take place between people or groups. It can also occur between countries.*

People and countries trade to get goods and services. These are usually things that they don't have or cannot make themselves. Sometimes one group has too much of something. It can sell these extra goods through trade.

Some countries are rich in natural **resources**. They may have coal or gold. Or their farmers may grow products, such as cotton and corn.

Other countries make goods in factories. Countries compete to sell their goods to other countries. They buy things they can't make themselves from other countries. They might also buy resources that they need.

A **market** is the space in which goods and services are bought and sold. A market can be defined by a physical location. For example, all the trade in a town is part of a local market. A market can also mean all the trade of a certain product around the world.

All **free markets** work according to the laws of supply and demand. Supply is how much of a product will be sold and at what price. Demand is how much of that product people will buy at a certain price. The price of a product depends on both the demand for it and how much there is of it.

Transportation and communication have improved over time. This has made international trade easier and faster.

Paying money in exchange for food at your school cafeteria is a form of trade.

Did You Know?

Native Americans had wide trading networks long before Europeans arrived. They traded goods such as salt, shells, furs, and copper. There is **evidence** that North Americans were in contact with South Americans.

The History of Trade

Trade is one of the earliest recorded human activities. Evidence has been found of trade that took place more than 150,000 years ago.

For thousands of years, trade worked on a **barter** system. To barter means to trade one kind of good for another. This is direct trade.

As societies became larger, the idea of money developed. Money can be whatever a society agrees on to represent a value. Beads, shells, or coins and bills can be used as money. Modern trade is usually **indirect** trade. This means that money is used to buy goods.

The Age of Exploration

In the 1400s and 1500s, Europeans wanted more gold, silver, and spices. This led to the Age of Exploration. Many of the first explorers were trying to find new trade routes. They wanted better ways to get to the riches of East Asia.

The spice trade helped create many European **colonies**. In time, these colonies won their independence. They became their own nations.

A hard, glass-like stone called obsidian was traded in the Stone Age.

Native Americans traded furs with European colonists in the 1600s.

The Silk Road was a trade route that existed more than 2,000 years ago. Starting from China, it stretched 4,000 miles. It ran across the Middle East and as far as Rome in Europe.

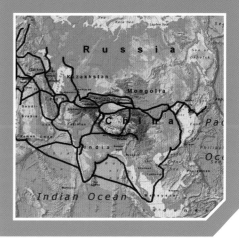

Tobacco and sugar were important trade goods in the American colonies.

If you trade your chicken's eggs for vegetables from your neighbor's garden, you are bartering.

Types of Trade

There are different types of trade. They depend on how many groups there are and where the goods are being traded.

Bilateral trade takes place between two people or groups. Multilateral trade includes more than two parties. Much of the world's trade is multilateral.

Domestic trade takes place within one country. International trade takes place between two or more countries. Many businesses sell their products both at home and in other countries. Selling into different markets helps them find new **consumers** for their products.

Imports and Exports

Goods and services brought into a country are called imports. Imports are usually things that a country doesn't have. Countries also import goods that other nations can make for less money. **Exports** are goods and services sold to other countries.

Almost anything can be traded. Both national and international markets trade a wide variety of products. Goods can range from staples to luxuries. Stocks and business services are also traded.

A wide range of services support trade. Businesses need insurance, communications, and transportation to succeed. In international trade, language translation is important.

Costs like transportation and insurance add to the price of traded goods.

Trade makes money for countries. It also creates jobs in packaging, transportation, and marketing.

Some developing nations have only one or two major exports. They are often crops, such as tea or coffee.

The U.S. exports a wide variety of goods and services. Some are resources such as ores and minerals. Others are **manufactured** goods such as cars and machinery. China, South Africa, Australia, and the U.S. mine much of the world's gold.

International Trade

Almost all countries trade with other countries. Very few nations have all the goods and resources that their citizens want and need.

Free Trade

Free trade is based on the removal of **tariffs**. Tariffs are taxes on imported goods. They support local industries by making imports more expensive. Tariffs make people buy their own country's products instead of imports.

People who support free trade believe tariffs should be removed. They argue that tariffs add to the cost of goods. They want to stop protecting industries.

Protectionism

Protectionism is the opposite of free trade. It puts up barriers to international trade to protect local companies and industries. Subsidies, tariffs, quotas, and tax cuts are forms of protectionism. For example, India has tariffs on wool and coal imports to their country. This allows their own farmers and miners to compete with imported products.

Some people believe that free trade damages the environment. With free trade, there are no limits on how much a country can export. People argue that natural resources will be used up faster.

If a country imports more than it exports, the country has a trade deficit. A trade surplus occurs when a country exports more than it imports.

Businesses **promote** their products in the international market. They go to trade fairs to sell their products to international buyers.

International businesspeople need to know about cultural differences. In Japan, it is important to exchange business cards before a meeting begins.

Countries used to trade mainly within their own regions. The United States' trading partners now range widely. Some are nearby neighbors, such as Canada and Mexico. Others are farther away, like China and Japan.

Canada is one of the U.S.' top trading partners. In 2006, the two countries did $533 billion in trade with each other.

Regulating International Trade

Governments and organizations control the buying and selling of goods and resources between countries.

Governments regulate trade through quotas, embargos, and tariffs. A quota is a limit to the amount of a good or resource that can be imported. An embargo blocks trade with a particular country. Embargoes are usually set up because of political differences.

Sometimes countries work together to form a trade organization. This is a group of countries that agree to charge less for each other's products. Working together gives them more power in the world's markets.

International trade is growing quickly. Worldwide organizations have been formed to help regulate it. The World Bank lends money to developing countries. The International Monetary Fund (IMF) oversees the world's financial markets.

World Trade Organization

The World Trade Organization (WTO) was set up in 1995. Its job is to supervise and encourage international trade. It increases international trade by lowering trade barriers and holding trade **negotiations**.

The North American Free Trade Agreement (NAFTA) began in 1994. It has removed many trade barriers between the United States, Canada, and Mexico.

OPEC (Organization of Petroleum Exporting Countries) is a trade organization. It was set up to protect the oil industry.

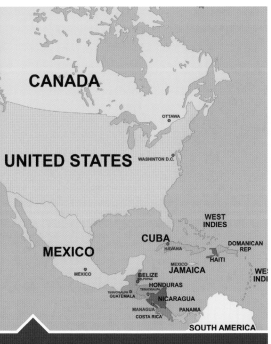

The U.S. has had a trade embargo against Cuba for over 45 years.

Did You Know?

The WTO headquarters are in Geneva, Switzerland. The WTO currently has 151 members. Its newest members are Vietnam and Tonga, which joined in 2007.

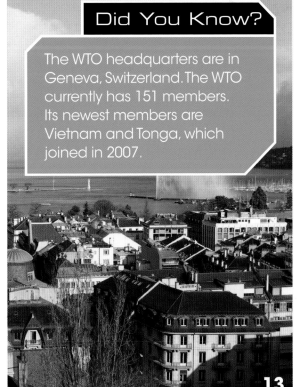

Interdependence

Countries tend to specialize in certain goods and services. This means they depend on other countries for everything else.

Most countries don't make all the goods and services that they need. Instead, they concentrate on making a few things. This is called specialization. The products that a country makes are usually based on the resources that it has.

When countries specialize, they must trade for the other things they need. They depend on other countries for staples like food and fuel. This interdependence can build ties between countries. But it can also cause problems when goods or services aren't available.

Measure Your Interdependence

Make a list of all the things you use in a day. Try to think of everything, from food to clothing to electronics. Then think about where these goods come from. Your clothing may have been made in the Philippines. Maybe your music player was made in Japan. Your food might have been grown in Asia or New Zealand. You can buy these things because of international trade.

One of the United States' biggest exports is motor vehicles. They also are one of its biggest imports.

We are used to being able to buy fresh fruits and vegetables year round. During the summer, many of them come from the U.S. But in the winter they may come from other places, such as Mexico or South America.

Video games are some of the many kinds of electronics that the United States imports from Asia.

In 2006, the U.S. imported $115 billion worth of electronics, like televisions and computers.

Problems Related to Trade

International trade involves many countries and large distances. Problems can arise. Many things can affect trade.

Trade Wars

International trade is very competitive. Disagreements can lead to trade wars. Countries use tariffs, quotas, and **bans** on certain imports to try to win a trade war. Both sides often lose trade as a result.

Health and Safety

Health and safety are important parts of international trading. Customs officials regulate the movement of animals and food products across borders. The increased threat of disease has made these checks even more important.

Bird flu is a disease that can pass from birds to humans. It has had a major effect on the trade of chickens and other birds. The disease has now been found in birds in dozens of countries. It could lead to trade bans and tougher rules for **quarantines.**

Terrorism

Another major problem facing the world today is the threat of terrorism. Huge numbers of products are traded internationally. Terrorists could use this movement of goods for their own purposes. Goods must be tightly controlled to prevent that.

Did You Know?

To be labeled *organic*, food must be grown and prepared in certain ways. Then customers know what they are buying.

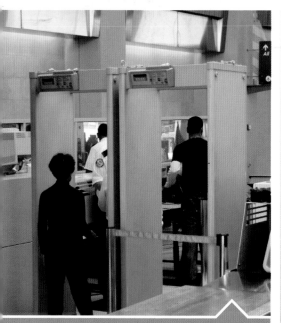

Customs officials use X-ray machines and trained dogs. They help keep dangerous items out of the country.

FOOT & MOUTH DISEASE PRECAUTION PLEASE STAY OFF LAND
THANK YOU

Many plant and animal species are protected. It is illegal to trade in products from protected animals, such as elephant tusks (ivory). However, these products are worth a lot of money. Smugglers are often tempted to break the law.

Case Study—Mad Cow Disease

In the 1980s, an illness called mad cow disease was found in British cattle. The disease had a huge effect on the world's beef markets.

Mad cow disease destroys brain and spine cells in cattle. It is also a serious problem for people. Scientists think it may be passed on to people who eat infected meat. When the disease was found, many countries banned British live beef imports. But they still imported British beef products. They were sold until it was found that they could also carry the disease.

In 2003 and 2006, infected animals were found in the United States. Japan is a major buyer of U.S. beef. It banned U.S. beef imports. Trade between the two countries has started again. However, Japan has very strict rules for importing U.S. beef.

Officials passed laws to stop the spread of the disease. But it took years for these laws to be introduced. Some people believe that the laws are not strict enough. They think mad cow disease may still be a threat to human health.

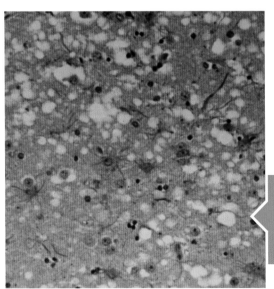

Mad cow disease causes small holes in cows' brains. It makes them look like sponges.

The scientific name for mad cow disease is bovine spongiform encephalopathy, or BSE. Scientists think it may cause the human disease variant Creutzfeld-Jacob Disease (vCJD). About 150 people have died from vCJD worldwide.

The British BSE outbreak killed more than 200,000 cows. Another 4.5 million healthy animals were destroyed to stop the disease from spreading.

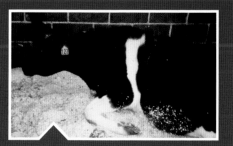

How Does Mad Cow Disease Spread?

BSE is spread when cows eat food that contains infected cattle parts. Cattle feed sometimes contained animal products. This led to the outbreak. Using animal products in cattle feed is now banned.

Unfair Trade Practices

International trade allows goods and resources to move around the world. This helps some countries more than others.

Many countries use tariffs and subsidies to help their own industries. But these practices can hurt poorer, developing countries. Subsidies are money that a nation gives to a certain industry, such as farming. Subsidies make that country's farm products cheaper. This can lead to large amounts of subsidized crops to end up on the international market.

Many developing countries depend on selling their surplus food internationally. They can't compete with the cheap subsidized goods.

Some companies move their factories to poorer countries.

There they can pay workers lower wages and make a bigger **profit**. In some factories, workers are not paid a good wage. Sometimes health and safety rules are ignored. These types of factories are called sweatshops. Child labor is also still a big problem. Children work in factories, on farms, or on the streets instead of going to school.

Make Trade Fair is an international organization set up to fight these problems. It encourages companies to buy goods directly from the people in developing countries. This means that the people get more money.

European subsidies in the 1970s and 1980s created problems. Heavily subsidized farmers made too much butter and milk. It couldn't all be sold and ended up rotting in storage.

Many types of coffee are now fairly traded.

The band Coldplay uses its fame to draw attention to the Make Trade Fair campaign.

WTO meetings often attract large groups of **protestors**. They say the WTO supports an unequal balance of power between rich and poor nations.

The Oil-for-Food Program

*The Oil-for-Food program showed how **corruption** affects international trade.*

The Gulf War

In 1990, Iraq invaded the neighboring country of Kuwait. This act started the Gulf War. The United Nations immediately placed **sanctions** on Iraq. They wanted to pressure the Iraqi leader, Saddam Hussein, to withdraw troops from Kuwait.

Oil-for-Food Program

People worried that Iraqi citizens were suffering because of the sanctions. The Oil-for-Food program was set up in 1995. This billion-dollar program allowed Iraq to sell its oil. But it could only sell oil to get food, medicine, and other basic goods. This was to stop Saddam Hussein from using oil money to buy weapons.

Corruption Problems

The program was successful in one way. It got necessary supplies to the Iraqi people. But some involved in the program were corrupt. People, companies, and even whole countries were part of it. They allowed the Iraqi government to still sell oil for money. The Iraqi government gave out bribes and received kickbacks. This allowed them to get around many of the controls.

Legal action related to the corruption continued until 2007. Even then, only a few people had been charged.

The Iraqi government illegally made $1.8 billion from the sale of oil.

The United Nations was responsible for the Oil-for-Food program. It has taken part of the blame for the corruption that occurred.

Did You Know?

The Australian Wheat Board was the largest payer of kickbacks to the Iraqi government. It paid them to guarantee the sale of Australian wheat in Iraq.

The Globalization of Culture

*Movies, television, and music are all part of popular culture. They show lifestyles and cultural **values**.*

Today many types of popular culture are traded through the global market. This encourages the exchange of cultures. It also leads to **globalization**. Supporters of cultural globalization say it helps cultures understand each other. They can then accept their differences. They say that both Eastern and Western cultures affect each other.

Globalization affects technology, music, movies, and other art forms. People can enjoy food, products, and ideas from other countries. They can take part in global sporting events, such as the Olympics.

However, people living in traditional cultures may not agree with different values. They may not want Western values to change their cultures. In the same way, Westerners may not like some values in foreign cultures. For example, India's caste system may go against beliefs about equality.

Some say that the exchange is too one-sided. They argue that Western values and culture are taking over all the others. They claim globalization is making other countries more like Western countries. They say this is because of the West's power in world trade.

The saying "it's a small world" is becoming a reality. Globalization is bringing people and cultures closer together.

Hip-hop music started off as the music of a small section of African-American society. It is now popular around the world.

Popular culture includes movies, music, television, newspapers, and books. It can even include clothing and accessories.

Modern communication can quickly spread news worldwide. Images of the 2004 Indian Ocean Tsunami were in our living rooms as it happened.

Trading Stocks

Investors trade stocks on both local and international stock markets. Stocks are shares of ownership in a business or company.

If a company does well, the value of its stock increases. If it does poorly, the value will decrease.

Money can be made from stocks in two ways. They are capital growth and dividends. Capital growth is when the value of the stock goes up. These shares can then be sold for a profit. Everyone who owns stock in a company receives dividends when a company does well. Dividends are the investors' shares of the profits.

Supply and Demand

Like other markets, stock markets are based on supply and demand. The price of a stock can go up or down many times a day. It is based on the demand for the stock and the amount available to buy at a given time.

Did You Know?

Many Internet-based companies started up during the 1990s. In 2000, the "dot-com bubble" burst, and stock prices plunged. Many companies did not survive.

Buying stocks in newer industries, such as Internet companies, is riskier than buying stocks in more established companies.

Many people buy stocks as investments. Stock trading on the Internet is very popular.

Blue chip stocks are shares in large, settled companies. They often provide low profits. But they are also dependable and low risk.

Money can be made and lost very quickly on the stock market. Knowing when to buy and sell is important.

OCA-COLA AMATIL   Net profit

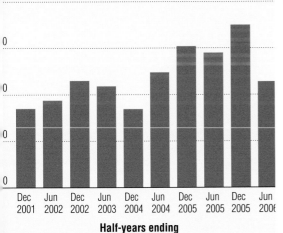

billions

Dec 2001	Jun 2002	Dec 2002	Jun 2003	Dec 2004	Jun 2004	Dec 2005	Jun 2005	Dec 2005	Jun 2006

Half-years ending

sults from 2004 prepared
der new IFRS accounting standards

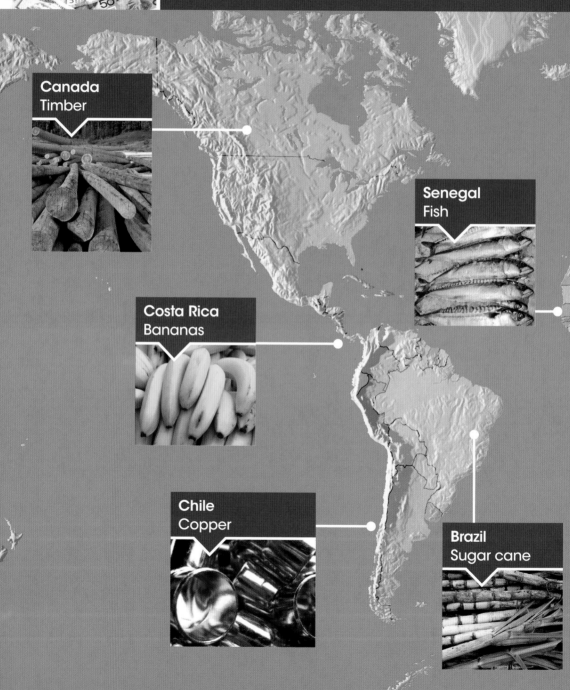

Canada
Timber

Senegal
Fish

Costa Rica
Bananas

Chile
Copper

Brazil
Sugar cane

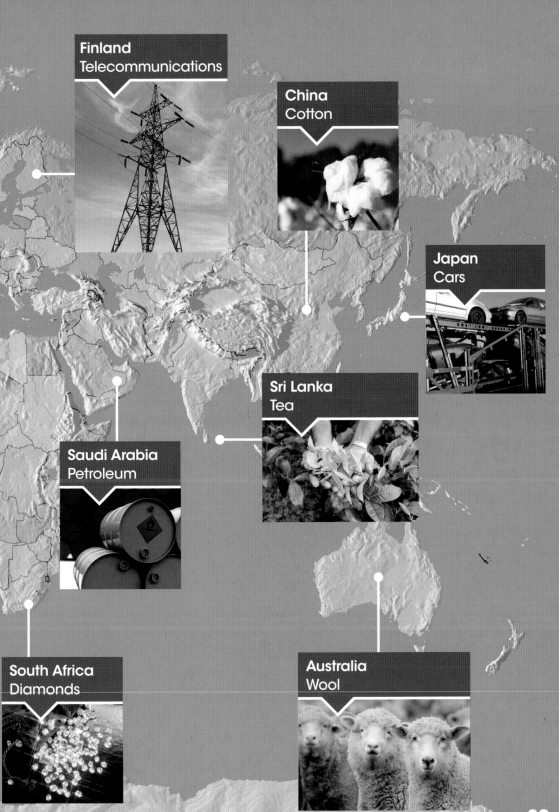

Finland
Telecommunications

China
Cotton

Japan
Cars

Sri Lanka
Tea

Saudi Arabia
Petroleum

South Africa
Diamonds

Australia
Wool

Trade Industries

Trade creates many jobs in support industries.

packaging

telecommunications

law enforcement

transport

tax administration

Trade

postal services

insurance

sales and marketing

banking

information technology

Glossary

bans (banz) laws or rules that do not allow something to be done

barter (BAHR tuhr) trade by directly exchanging goods or services rather than using money

colonies (KOL uh neez) areas of land under the control of another country

consumers (kuhn SOO muhrz) people who use goods or services

corruption (kuh RUHP shuhn) an act or acts of dishonesty

evidence (EHV uh duhns) information that makes it reasonable to believe something is true

exports (EHKS pohrts) goods made in one country that are sent to another country to be sold

free markets (FREE   MAHR kihts) markets where prices are set through free competition between businesses

globalization (GLOH buhl uh ZAY shuhn) the process of goods and services becoming more similar around the world; can affect societies and cultures

goods (gudz) things that are made that can be bought and owned

indirect (IHN duh REHKT) not directly connected; secondary

investors (ihn VEHS tuhrz) people who put money into things, such as stocks, that they hope will be worth more in the future

manufactured (MAN yuh FAK chuhrd) made by hand or by machine

market (MAHR kiht) a place, which may or may not be physical, where buyers and sellers meet to exchange goods and services

negotiations (nih GOH shee AY shuhnz) talks to decide the terms of an agreement, such as for trade

profit (PROF iht) the difference between what something is sold for and the amount paid to make or buy it

promote (pruh MOHT) to encourage the sales of a product through advertising or other activities

protestors (PROH tehs tuhrz) people who object to something in a public way, such as making signs and marching

quarantines (KWAWR uhn teenz) procedures that keep people, animals, or plants away from everything else for a limited time to make sure they don't carry diseases

resources (REE sohrs ehz) the materials, skills, or money that a person or country can use to make or do things

sanctions (SANGK shuhnz) actions taken by the international community to get a country do something, usually by withholding trade

services (SUR vihs ehz) work that people can buy that doesn't create a physical product

tariffs (TAR ihfs) taxes charged by governments on imported and exported goods

values (VAL yooz) the beliefs and customs that are important to a person, group, or culture

Index